FORGIVEN TO FORGIVE

or
The Cancer of Bitterness

William J. Finnigan

ISBN 1-56632-097-6

Copyright © 1995 by Revival Literature. All rights reserved. No reproduction in any form of this book, in whole or in part, except for brief quotations in articles or reviews, may be made without written permission from Revival Literature, P. O. Box 6068, Asheville, NC 28816.

Printed in the United States of America.

Contents

The Cancer of Bitterness 5

The Cause of Bitterness 8

The Curse of Bitterness 10

The Cure for Bitterness 20

FORGIVEN TO FORGIVE

or

The Cancer of Bitterness

It doesn't take an expert to conclude that we live in a society which has lost its way. Medical science and space technology continue to extend life on earth and beyond, while war, crime, and murder ravage the population. What kind of insanity has overtaken us? Where are the values and principles of integrity that once held us together?

We live in a society that seemingly has so much, yet in reality has so little. Not only do the homeless drift, but people of means grope without purpose through the maze of this life. Why am I here? Where did I come from? Where am I going? These are valid questions which strike the hearts of thinking people who are increasingly fearful of facing what appears to be a hopeless and uncertain future.

On top of everything else, people are laden with feelings of guilt, inferiority, emptiness and rejection. Multitudes run to mental health centers and prescription counters for relief, only to find that legitimate drugs are not much more effective than the illegitimate. We are a generation of pill poppers for all occasions, yet we are still on the search for peace and contentment.

I believe the foremost need of the inward man is acceptance and forgiveness. There is so much talk these days about "dysfunctional families," a term which infers that parents are less than perfect. Judged upon this basis, every family on earth is "dysfunctional." Surely, love and acceptance ought to be demonstrated in family life, but what if that is not the case—do we blame our parents, our environment, or our economic status? If these factors have caused our sense of rejection and low self-esteem, as many psychologists propound, then we have no hope of ever being different. Why? Because we cannot go back and change the past, or our parents!

Man is in a dilemma, having been made by God and yet, because of sin, being out of communion with God. Thus, the loving forgiveness, joy, and peace that God alone can impart are absent from rebellious man. In his guilt and emptiness he can only attempt to find relief in the so-called pleasures and toys of this world. Is it any wonder people turn to drugs, illicit sex, and money in an effort to quell fear and guilt? Tragically, however, this road leads to suicide, whether suddenly or slowly by the route of addiction.

Forgiveness is a wonderful thing. How tremendous it is to hear the words, "I forgive you" come from the lips of a loved one you have offended. How much greater it is to experience God's forgiveness and to know that you belong to Him forever. This can become a reality because God, and God alone, has made it possible.

The forgiving grace of God is pictured beautifully in the Old Testament book of Leviticus, chapter 16. Herein is portrayed the Day of Atonement, or *Yom Kippur*, which became the day of Israel's national cleansing from sin. The word *atonement* (*Kaphar*) has the idea of covering sin from the face of God by the shedding of innocent animal blood. Thus, the term means to reconcile man to God (literally: *at-one-ment*).

The ceremony on the Day of Atonement was conducted by Aaron the High Priest who selected two goats to be symbols of God's forgiveness of the people. In representation of his sin and that of Israel, Aaron placed his hands on the goat's head which signified a transference of sin to the innocent animal. Immediately the goat's throat was slit and blood pulsed out, silently crying, "Your sin is forgiven and cleansed by this innocent sacrifice—repent and believe!"

If that were not enough, a second goat was secured and again sin was imputed to the goat as the High Priest laid his hands upon him. Strangely, yet significantly, this animal was released into the wilderness, never to return. This goat became known as the Scapegoat, which symbolically carried away all the sins of Israel. Thus, the definition of "forgiveness" is beautifully expressed, namely, "to send away or cancel debt."

How wondrously this points to the One named Jesus Christ, Who became that innocent blood Sacrifice on the Cross. Christ became our Atonement for sin, not only in the cleansing and debt-cancelling aspect, but in that He removed our transgressions from us as far as the east is from the west. Hallelujah!

THE CAUSE OF BITTERNESS

Forgiveness is a primary characteristic of God, for the Psalmist said, "For thou, Lord, art good, and ready to forgive; and plenteous in mercy unto all them that call upon thee."[1] God alone is the Author of forgiveness. That was ultimately and clearly demonstrated through the sacrifice of His Son, "in whom we have redemption, [deliverance] through his blood, even the forgiveness of sins."[2]

On this basis, the believer in Christ has access to the ongoing work of God's forgiveness: "If we confess our sins, he is faithful and just to forgive us our sins, and to cleanse us from all unrighteousness."[3] What a tremendous promise to the grieving heart that has failed to obey his Father's demands.

Yet in light of the above truth, so many believers are still riddled with guilt and an unforgiving spirit. Why? Because they won't forgive God or others who have offended them. About 99 percent of the people I counsel are bitter about something or someone. Upon further examination, it becomes clear that their main issue is with the Lord Himself.

Before you consider this to be unthinkable in your case, take time to think it through. Have you ever said in your heart, if not with your mouth, "It isn't fair, Lord." Perhaps you have asked, "Why me, Lord?" or, "I prayed, God, and you didn't answer—where were you?" Oh, we don't like to admit this openly because it doesn't fit the cliché we hear so often during testimony time at the church, i.e., "God *always* answers my prayers." Our mouths often do not match our hearts, and the resulting conflict easily spawns a root of resentment and discouragement.

This is all part of Satan's age-old strategy to create discontentment in man's heart toward the sovereign person and purpose of God. Adam's basic sin was not the eating of a piece of fruit but the inward rejection of God's authority over his life. Adam's son Cain carried the same torch when he became "wroth" (angry) at God's command. Significantly, Cain's "countenance fell." That is, his bitter heart toward God produced a long face, indicating his depressed spirit.

This anger was further complicated when Cain slew his godly brother Abel as a rebellious blood "sacrifice." He wanted to kill God, but he couldn't get hold of Him. Thus, he settled for Abel, God's representative, until thousands of years later when the "cainites" finally committed deicide at the Cross.

The above scenario illustrates the cause and curse of depression—namely *bitterness*. This "disease" is prevalent not only in the world at large, but also among God's saints. This sin destroys individual lives as well as family and church relationships. In this regard, the Bible offers a weighty admonition: "Follow peace with all men . . . lest any root of bitterness springing up trouble you, and thereby many be defiled."[4]

Seeds of resentment and bitterness find lodging in human hearts, springing up into a full-bloomed harvest of depression and damaging addictions such as smoking, drugs, alcohol, and gambling. Psychologists and mental health experts are busy counseling these disturbed individuals, but ultimate answers seem unattainable and the epidemic continues to soar.

THE CURSE OF BITTERNESS

Bitterness or resentment when allowed to continue in a believer's life results in at least three serious consequences: 1) paralysis of faith; 2) prevention of God's forgiveness, and 3) a plague upon the physical body.

Let's consider these three factors.

First, bitterness will paralyze a person's ability to exercise faith, or authority, in God's Word.

In Mark 11:22-25, having just cursed the fig tree, Jesus exhorted the disciples, "Have faith in God. For . . . whosoever shall say unto this mountain, Be thou removed, and be thou cast into the sea; and shall not doubt in his heart, but shall believe that those things . . . shall come to pass, he shall have whatsoever he saith. Therefore . . . What things soever ye desire, when ye pray, believe that ye receive them, and ye shall have them. And when ye stand praying, forgive, if ye have ought against any. . . ."

Faith and effective prayer presuppose the believer's ongoing fellowship with God and his joyful submission to God's will. Faith not only prays but *says* to mountains of authority, "Be thou thou removed!" A critical, fruitless, and resentful spirit is not conducive to such faith.

The Pharisees of Jesus' day were a legalistic, critical, bitter, and fruitless people. The cursing of the fig tree was a classic demonstration to illustrate these pharisaical attitudes. Thus, Jesus challenged the disciples to maintain a clear and effective prayer channel, unhindered by unbelief.

What is it that kills, or paralyzes our faith? It is an unforgiving spirit. "When ye stand praying, forgive. . . . " Hatred is the *cain spirit* that sours the human race and unfortunately robs too many saints from taking authority over the world, the flesh, and the devil.

Of all that attacks the believer in Christ, there are two areas that appear the most devastating. Drugs, alcohol and sex are not the most addictive, as difficult as these may seem. In John 8:44, Jesus again addresses the Pharisees, making it clear that they are the spiritual offspring of Satan. "Ye are of your father the devil, and the lusts of your father ye will do. He was a *murderer* from the beginning, and abode not in the truth, because there is no truth in him. . . . He is a *liar*, and the father of it."*

Note that Satan is a *murderer* and a *liar*. These two areas, in my opinion, are the most difficult for the believer to overcome. Satan hates us with destructive passion and has determined that we hate everyone except him. We all seem to carry resentment and hurt feelings from our earliest years and even the new birth does not necessarily nullify these wounds. As we shall see later, the quickest way to give Satan access to our inner lives is through resentment and bitterness.

As *the* liar, Satan hates *the* Truth (Jesus Christ) and delights in deceiving us concerning the fantasy island around us, namely, the world. This is make-believe land; don't be too enamored by it. The real world is revealed in God's Word, the Bible. Only God can make us "real" people, being "true-blue," or faithful to God and one another.

Therefore, hatred, or a murderous spirit, can paralyze our faith and further allow Satan to set up a stronghold in our minds. I believe that many of the habits, such as smoking and drinking, that continue to haunt the saints can be traced back to a root of bitterness (the stronghold).

Remember, David said, "If I regard iniquity

in my heart, the Lord will not hear me."[5] Thus, it is imperative that we keep our hearts free from bitterness if we are to enjoy the fruitfulness and power of God. A wrong attitude results in wrong living and wrong praying, which can only result in a power-shortage before God and men.

Bitterness or resentment will not only paralyze our faith, but secondly, it will prevent the experience of God's forgiveness.

Jesus emphasized clearly that, "When ye stand praying, forgive, if ye have ought against any: that your Father also which is in heaven may forgive you your trespasses. But if ye do not forgive, neither will your Father . . . forgive your trespasses."[6] Many of God's people are not enjoying the fullness of His forgiveness because they are harboring unforgiveness toward others. It is assumed that because one is born again the ongoing experience of personal forgiveness is automatic. According to Jesus' words, that is a false assumption.

In what is commonly called the Lord's Prayer, this truth is further reiterated. Jesus is teaching His disciples to pray thus: "Our Father which art in heaven. . . . Give us this day our daily bread. And *forgive us* our debts, *as we forgive* our debtors." (See Matt. 6:9-12.)

We are taught here to expect God's forgiveness only as we forgive those who trespass, or sin, against us. In fact, Jesus further states the issue concretely in verses 14 and 15, "For if ye forgive men their trespasses, your heavenly Father will also forgive you: But if ye forgive not men their trespasses, neither will your Father forgive your trespasses."

Luke's rendering of Jesus' words displays the

positive attitude of saving grace: "And forgive us our sins; for we also forgive everyone that is indebted to us." (Luke 11:4) It's like now that we are forgiven, our total forgiveness of others is only the natural (or supernatural) way to go—and it is.

Everyone has a problem with forgiving others. Even the great apostle Peter struggled with this issue when he approached Jesus and asked Him how many times he must forgive an offending brother. "Till seven times?" he asked. (See Matt. 18:21f.) Seven being the "perfect" number, Peter evidently thought that forgiving another up to seven times was the ultimate sacrifice. Jesus, however, retorted, "Not ... Until seven times: but, Until seventy times seven." (v. 22)

Knowing Peter, he probably took out his calculator, punched in 70x7=490 and asked, "You mean on the 491st time I can give him what he deserves?"

Sound familiar? That's the typical response of the human heart untouched with a sense of God's forgiving grace. At that point, Jesus expounded to Peter possibly the most powerful and revealing parable in the Scriptures pertaining to the subject of forgiveness. Please take time to read and ponder this passage in Matt. 18:23-35.

Briefly summarized, the parable speaks of a certain king who decides to take account of all debts owed him by his servants. One owed the king ten thousand talents, or approximately ten million dollars. When brought into accountability, the grieved servant falls down and worships (begs) him, saying, "Lord, have patience with me, and I will pay thee all." (v. 26) Wonder of wonders, the king is moved with compassion and forgives him (cancels) the debt.

The plot thickens, however, as the forgiven servant leaves and meets a fellow servant who owes him a hundred pence, or about twenty dollars. You would think that after the tremendous deliverance just experienced by the first servant that he would testify of the king's marvelous, forgiving grace, and tell the second servant to forget the twenty dollars.

Sorry to say, however, that's not the way it happened.

Instead, the first servant lays hold of the second, grabbing him by the throat, saying, "Pay me that thou owest." (lit. "Pay me, pay me, pay me!)[7] The victim falls to his knees and literally cries for mercy just like the first servant had done before the king. (v. 29) Guess what kind of response he receives? Jesus tells us, "And he *would not*: but went and cast him into prison, till he should pay the debt." (v. 30)

What an incredible reaction by a forgiven servant toward another servant seeking his forgiveness. Why couldn't the first servant freely have mercy on the second, especially when he had just experienced the full release of the king for an immeasurable debt? This travesty of justice is incomprehensible unless you understand the deep, dark depravity of the human heart.[8] Unfortunately, it happens every day among believers and unbelievers alike.

Word of the incident gets back to the king who in righteous anger rebukes the unforgiving servant with these piercing words, "O thou wicked servant, I forgave thee all that debt, because thou desiredst me; shouldest not thou also have had compassion on thy fellowservant, even as I had pity on thee?"[9]

Note that the king delivers this servant to the "tormentors."[10] Jesus goes on to say, "So likewise shall my heavenly Father do also unto you, if ye *from your hearts* forgive not every one his brother their trespasses." (v. 35)

Christians do not automatically enjoy forgiveness. We must be conscious of our relationship with God and with others. I'm afraid many believers are suffering from a lack of personal forgiveness because they are holding grudges and hard feelings toward others.

Some may hide behind the sentiment, "Well, I can forgive, I just can't forget." But Jesus said it's a heart matter over which He will give grace if we deal with it properly. He didn't mean that the offense would never cross our memory again, but rather because of forgiving grace the thought of the offense will never disturb us again. That is, the stinger of bitterness will be removed and we will be free to once again look our offenders straight in the eye with the absence of all malice. Amen!

Bitterness will not only *paralyze* our faith and *prevent* God's forgiveness, it will become a *plague* to our physical well-being. I'm convinced that much of bodily disease these days is triggered, not by bacteria, but by bitterness.

You see, what fills your mind is what eventually spills out into your body and behavior. Pent up anger or bitterness is epidemic in society. Though anger can be a positive emotion (e.g., righteous indignation), prolonged, unwarranted anger is physically destructive. Dr. Redford Williams of Duke University Medical Center makes the following observation: "Anger stimulates the release of the hormones adrenaline and cortisol into the bloodstream. These two hormones have a number of effects that mobilize the body over the short term but that can be destructive if arousal is chronic."[11]

He goes on to discuss several of the devastating results that may develop when these hormones are perpetually released into the body. He says:

- The hormones cause heart rate and blood pressure to rise. This can damage the delicate inner lining of the arteries and accelerate the development of arteriosclerosis—a buildup of plaque that can lead to a heart attack.

- They cause platelets circulating in the blood to become sticky. That enables them to cling to damaged areas on the artery lining, where they clump and ... further stimulate the growth of plaque.

- They stimulate fat cells to empty into the bloodstream to provide quick energy. When that fat isn't burned, it is converted into cholesterol—making more ... available ... plaque.

- They appear to suppress the immune system, making us more susceptible to illness.[12]

These recent medical observations should not surprise us, seeing that God's Word spoke to the issue long before modern medicine. Worthy of our consideration in this regard is the weighty passage of Prov. 3:5-8, "Trust in the Lord with all thine heart; and lean not unto thine own understanding. In all thy ways acknowledge Him, and He shall direct thy paths. Be not wise in thine own eyes: fear the LORD, and depart from evil. It shall be health to thy navel, and marrow to thy bones."[13]

An unforgiving spirit is in direct opposition to everything portrayed in the above admonition. One who is angry and bitter *is* leaning on his own understanding, trying to analyze why he's been treated so wrongly. He's certainly not trusting God in the matter, because in his thinking God had something to do with his dilemma. That's right. I'm saying that the bitter spirit has an issue with God Himself!

The believer who has an issue with God cannot trust, or confide in God. No one goes for advice to a counselor with whom he has a controversy. That's why so often we run *from* our gracious Father instead of *to* Him. We must understand this fact if we're going to experience deliverance over bitterness.

The passage under consideration further exhorts us to "fear the LORD, and depart from evil." Fearing God, simply put, means taking God and His Word seriously. It's really another definition of "trust" or "faith." Heb. 11:7 says, "By faith Noah, being warned of God of things not seen as yet, *moved with fear*, prepared an ark. . . ." If we fear God and depart from evil (e.g., resentment, bitterness, etc.) then we can experience God's fulfillment and the peace that passes all understanding.

In fact, the Proverb writer strongly infers that if we truly walk in the fear of God then we can be free of all the other fears (paranoia, worry, etc.)

that seem to plague so many in our day. Plus, he says that this walk of faith "shall be health (literally: *healing*) to thy navel, and marrow to thy bones." Being right with God and others can greatly enhance our bodily health.

On the contrary, a bitter, unforgiving spirit can reap great havoc on the body, as has been already expressed in Dr. William's article. In addition, the above Scripture correlates inner faith with physical soundness. The navel, or umbilicus, speaks of our abdomen where the emotion of pain and suffering is located. Ulcers and colitis are not uncommon among those harboring fear and resentment.

Bone marrow is not only essential to our skeletal structure, it is also responsible for the production of red blood cells. The word *marrow* carries the idea of *moisture*, without which the bones become brittle and dried. Prov. 14:30 says, "A sound heart [mind] is the life [health] of the flesh [body]: but envy the rottenness of the bones." I have little question after many years of counseling, that prolonged envy and resentment can trigger crippling arthritis and other bone diseases.[14]

* * *

This discussion would not be complete without considering the role of "the tormentors" whom Jesus mentioned in the previously addressed parable about forgiveness. (Matt. 18:34) While a true believer can never be demon possessed, he can become a victim of depression, obsession and even oppression.[15] I can tell you that there is no quicker way to bring on these torments than to harbor a bitter spirit.

We are exhorted in Eph. 4:27 not to "give place to the devil." Evidently that's possible for a believer to do. A perusal of the context will reveal, among other things, the sin of bitterness. Verse 26 says, "Let not the sun go down upon your wrath." In other words, deal with your pent up anger before you go to bed or else expect the devil to take the opportunity to create havoc. Paul goes on to say, "Let no corrupt communication proceed out of your mouth, but that which is good to the use of edifying, that it may minister grace unto the hearers. And grieve not the holy Spirit of God, whereby ye are sealed unto the day of redemption. Let all bitterness, and wrath, and anger, and clamour, and evil speaking, be put away from you, with all malice: And be ye kind one to another, tenderhearted, forgiving one another, even as God for Christ's sake hath forgiven you." (Eph. 4:29-32)

Briefly stated, bitterness grieves the God of all forgiveness and opens the door for demonic tormentors to victimize the saint, affecting his inner life and testimony. Satan, the propagator of hate and destruction, still desires to sift us as wheat and keep us under the curse of bitterness. But, praise be to God, there is a cure.

* * *

Before addressing the remedy for bitterness, I would like to ask several reflective and pointed questions regarding Jesus' teaching on the subject:

1. How is it that the King forgives but slaves won't?

2. How can such tremendous debt (e.g., 10 million dollars) be forgiven, when small or lesser

debts go unforgiven?

3. Why can't forgiven sinners forgive forgiven sinners? How can this be, especially when the holy, sinless God forgives sinners? One can only conclude biblically that an unforgiving spirit reveals an ignorance and/or the absence of God's saving grace.

THE CURE FOR BITTERNESS

The remedy can only begin through the Holy Spirit using His Word to reveal and convict the murderous sin of bitterness in one's life. As stated in the introduction, all individuals are born under Satan's domain (John 8:44), thus manifesting his murderous (hateful) spirit in various degrees. God alone has the remedy—"For the Word of God is quick, and powerful, and sharper than any two-edged sword, piercing even to the dividing asunder of soul and spirit, and of the joints and marrow, and is a discerner of the thoughts and intents of the heart." (Heb. 4:12)

Meditate carefully upon the above Scripture because it is the key that unlocks the door of freedom for those held by sin. It is the *Word* and only the *Word* that's "sharper than any two-edged sword [scalpel] . . . piercing even . . . the soul and spirit." We're talking about Divine surgery in an area that nothing in this world can touch. You may temporarily tranquilize the effects of sin with drugs, liquor, smoking, sex, or money, but you can never reach the root cause of sin with these.

Giving a shot of morphine to a cancer patient may ease the pain for a time but it does nothing for the cancer. Sin is a cancer and getting drunk may create a false euphoria, or "high," but it soon vanishes when sobriety returns. That person then must look for a higher high to offset the lower low, until he OD's or dies. This is the plight of man without God.

It is the Word, therefore, in the hand of the Great Physician that can heal the sin-sick soul. Since bitterness opens the door for a demonic stronghold in the mind, only a remedy that reaches the soul can bring deliverance. Substance abuse is not the root problem, but only an outward manifestation emanating from the inner stronghold of bitterness. These substances enter and leave the body, effecting the brain, but they can never penetrate the stronghold. This is why people can go from Alcoholics Anonymous to Narcotics Anonymous to Smokers Anonymous and never get full and permanent release from the real problem, sin.

No wonder Satan vehemently opposes the Word of God for he knows more than most the miraculous healing power it is for man's spirit, soul and body. Not only does the Word operate on the inner life (soul and spirit), but also on *the joints and marrow*. Yes, when there is forgiveness and deliverance in the soul it has a profound influence on the physical body. As we have previously discussed, bitterness and anger can cripple us physically. But thanks be to God Who can do today what He did in the wilderness when "He sent his word, and healed them, and delivered them from their destructions." (Psa. 107:20) I have personally witnessed physical healing in folks who have dealt scripturally with their sin of bitterness.

My friend, has the message of this booklet brought uneasiness and guilt to your soul? Are you convinced that you are a sinner before a Holy God with no way to escape His judgment? Could it be that you have never repented of your sin and by faith acknowledged Jesus Christ as your Lord and personal Saviour? Dear one, if this is so, there is no better time than *now* to cry out to this great God Who says, "Come unto me, all ye that labour and are heavy laden, and I will give you rest. . . . For whosoever shall call upon the name of the Lord shall be saved." (Matt. 11:28; Rom. 10:13) Just stop right here, dear sinner friend, and with bowed head, ask the Lord Jesus Christ to save your soul *now*.

Probably most who read this message are professing Christians who testify of saving faith in Christ. However, the Spirit of God has brought uneasiness and guilt to your soul as well. You know that you have maligned others with your mouth and harbored resentment in your heart. These ill feelings may extend all the way back to childhood and you may have never dealt with them in a scriptural manner.

Saint, are you willing to deal with your bitterness, or will you deny its existence in your life, even though God has brought conviction to your heart? I tell you, Satan will battle you ferociously at this point because he knows the potential freedom that comes when his stronghold is destroyed in the believer's mind and is replaced by a flood tide of God's power and glory.

Don't let the enemy deceptively talk you out of this decision. Face the issue squarely and do it *now*! Let me suggest at least six steps toward the God-given cure for bitterness:

1. Take full responsibility for your sin. In other words, stop blaming others for your problem. We live in a day when most people dodge their responsibility. They use their past and present circumstances, their parents, etc., as excuses for their dilemma. Don't do this! Remember, you stand alone before God, totally responsible for *your* attitude and actions.

2. Confess and repent of all bitterness toward God. Confession is literally "saying the same thing God says." That is, I'm agreeing with God about my sin. He says: "Bill, you've had a murderous, bitter spirit against Jim for years." I say, "Yes, Lord, I have had a murderous, bitter spirit against Jim for years." You let it all out before God—that's confession.

To repent is not only agreeing with God about my sin, but standing with God in His offense and grief over my sin. King David, with a broken spirit, cried in Psa. 51:2-4, "Wash me throughly from mine iniquity, and cleanse me from my sin. For I acknowledge my transgressions: and my sin is ever before me. *Against thee, thee only* have I sinned, and done this evil in thy sight: that thou mightest be justified . . . when thou judgest."

You see, repentance is not only my grief and God's grief over my sin, but a "change of mind" about sin. In other words, I'm determined by God's grace to make a break with this sin and maintain a clear, forgiving heart. Amen!

3. Claim God's forgiveness. When you have cried out to God in repentant faith, don't let the "accuser of our brethren" (Rev. 12:10) talk you out of God's sweet forgiveness. This anger and bitterness runs so deeply that one can be convinced that he's committed the unpardonable sin. Don't accept that notion, but rather cling in faith to the Word which says, "If we confess our sins, he is faithful and just to forgive us our sins, and to cleanse us from all unrighteousness. . . . Seek ye the LORD while he may be found, call ye upon him while he is near: Let the wicked forsake his way, and the unrighteous man his thoughts: and let him return unto the LORD, and he will have mercy upon him; and to our God, for he will abundantly pardon." (I John 1:9; Isa. 55:6-7)

It is essential that you drop all of your sin at the foot of the Cross. Christ paid the debt for your murderous, angry spirit, therefore, ask Him to remove that heavy burden and cleanse your guilty heart. Thank Him now for His marvelous, forgiving grace.

4. In prayer, forgive everyone who has ever offended you. I suggest you compose a list. It won't take long, for these will be the folks who have *hurt* you over the years and their names are still fresh in your mind. Yes, these are the ones you'd like to get rid of, if you could, or at least you hope that you will never see them again. You know who they are, don't you?

I exhort you now to bow your heart in prayer and forgive each one by name. You might pray thusly:

"Dear Father, as I have claimed Your forgiveness for my bitterness toward You and others, I choose now to forgive those individuals who have offended me. I may not feel like forgiving them, but I will to do it by faith. Thus I bring my brother Tom before You, and right now I choose to forgive him for all he's done to me. (Be specific.) Next, there are my parents whom I've blamed for things beyond their control and mine. Then there is Pastor Smith whom I've resented for years . . . " (Work through the entire list this way.)

The other side to this is also getting right with those whom *you* have offended. Jesus spoke to the issue in Matt. 5:23-24, "If thou bring thy gift to the altar, and there rememberest that thy brother hath ought against thee; leave there thy gift . . . and go thy way; first be reconciled to thy brother, and then come and offer thy gift."

We need to deal with those who have offended us and those whom we have offended. If someone has an issue with you, make the attempt to settle it with that person. (For further instruction in confronting others, refer to step six.)

5. **Take back the place given to Satan.** Since hatred and bitterness are so akin to Satan's character (John 8:44), he readily takes advantage of the bitter saint's open door policy. (Eph. 4:27) In fact, it's very possible that the stronghold of bitterness has been passed down to us from previous generations. The Lord says, "I the LORD thy God am a jealous God, visiting the iniquity of the fathers upon the children unto the third and fourth generation of them that hate me." (Exod. 20:5)

This thing is deep. Even beyond confession and repentance, we must consider taking back this ground from the enemy of our souls. By that, I mean a verbal renunciation—in and through the mighty name of Jesus Christ commanding the enemy to vacate the place he's held. This may all sound strange to the reader, but please bear with me in this critical moment. It is right here that a decisive victory must be won, for Satan will go to great lengths to confuse or hide the issue. Listen to the Apostle John's words as he describes Satan's defeat and the triumph of God's saints, "And the great dragon was cast out [of Heaven], that old serpent, called the Devil, and Satan, which deceiveth the whole world: he was cast out into the earth, and his angels were cast out with him. And I heard a loud voice saying in heaven, Now is come salvation, and strength, and the kingdom of our God, and the power of his Christ: for the accuser of our brethren is cast down, which accused them before our God day and night. And they *overcame* him by the blood of the Lamb, and by the word of their testimony; and they loved not their lives unto the death."[16]

Dear reader, take time right now and meditate upon this passage, for herein is the glorious key to freedom from the cancer of bitterness. Satan's stronghold must go because Jesus "was manifested, that he might destroy the works of the devil." (I John 3:8) This great work was accomplished once and for all at the Cross and the tomb. Therefore, as children of God we overcome him (Satan) "by the blood of the Lamb"—that's our birthright in the Lord Jesus Christ. Do you believe that? If so, are you ready to act upon that truth by faith?

John goes on to say, that "they overcame him ... by the *word of their testimony*...." This is critical, because he's talking about the saint's verbal and personal declaration of Christ's victory over Satan. This is not referring to one's giving a "testimony" of God's goodness during a Sunday night service, though certainly that's in order. Rather, this is a clear and definite renunciation of *any* place that Satan has gained in the believer's life.

James puts it this way: "Submit yourselves therefore to God. Resist the devil, and he will flee from you." (James 4:7) He did not simply say, "Resist sin," but he speaks of addressing the enemy. I know that Jude refers to Michael the archangel, who when contending with the devil said, "The Lord rebuke thee." (v. 9) But remember that we are not angels, but redeemed saints of God, standing in the authority of our Triumphant Overcomer.

Don't let the accuser pour doubt over your spirit at this point. He is a defeated foe, and he knows it. He just doesn't want you to know it nor to act upon that knowledge. So let's get on with the renunciation, that is, the taking back of the place that Satan has held in your life and then releasing that same place to the full possession of the Lord Jesus Christ. Are you ready?

Just vocalize this renunciation in faith: "I renounce you, Satan, in the matchless name of Jesus Christ Who is my Lord. I take back the ground (place) that I have given you through the sin of bitterness. (Mention any other sin here). I renounce any hold or curse that you have had over my life through my ancestors (parents, grandparents, etc.), and I declare freedom from such through the power and blood of the Lord Jesus Christ. Get behind me, Satan. You no longer have any place in my life. I hereby give the place that you once held to my Lord and Saviour Jesus Christ, Who defeated you once and for all on the Cross."

Then pray: "Dear Heavenly Father, I thank You, in Jesus' name, for your great victory over Satan and sin. I have confessed my bitterness to You and now I present to You the place that Satan once held in my life. Would you please take this place and fill it with your presence, power, and word. Fill me right now, dear Lord, with your Holy Spirit—from the top of my head to the bottom of my feet. Teach me how to walk daily in the Spirit, to obey Your Word, and to use it effectively against sin and Satan. Thank you for Your great deliverance through the blood sacrifice of Your Son. Please use me as an instrument of salvation to those who cross my path. In Jesus' mighty name, I pray."

6. Make restitution where needed. Most of the above steps thus far have been directed toward God. But remember that the Cross is not only vertical, it is also horizontal. Our relationship to God *always* effects those around us. Therefore, if I confess stealing money from my neighbor, God forgives me, but He then expects me to make it right with the neighbor.[17]

Begin praying for those toward whom you were previously embittered. Claim God's healing over any resentment and pray for His leadership in contacting these people. Don't let the enemy scare you at this point. God will lead you, not drive you. The Lord will lay on your heart the ones with whom He wants you to speak. He will even give you the words to say, so don't panic.

The best way to deal with people is face to face so expressions and gestures can be observed. If that isn't possible, then use the telephone, or a letter (in that order). Simply stated, you may say: (for example) "Sue, I want to share something very important with you. God has shown me that I've had resentment or hard feelings (bitterness) toward you; I have been dead wrong and have confessed my sin to the Lord. Would you please forgive me for my attitude and offense toward you?"

Wait for an answer. If the person responds affirmatively, sobeit. If they don't respond as you anticipated, don't be shocked. Remember, the reason for your restitution was to clear your soul before God and man. God will have to work in their hearts too, so just do what God made clear to you.

By the way, if the person you've offended has since died, there is nothing you can do personally. Do what you are now able to do and enjoy the great release of God in your soul. God bless you.

* * *

In closing, let me cite two biblical illustrations which epitomize the power of forgiveness. First, you remember Job's plight of physical suffering and disease, agitated by the nagging criticism of his wife and friends. Having developed an obvious resentment toward them, Job finds himself in an awesome confrontation with God Himself.

It is clear that Job repents of his attitude and humbles himself before the Lord. "And the Lord turned the captivity of Job, when he prayed for his friends." (Job 42:10) In other words, God delivered Job from his affliction when he was willing to forgive and pray for those who had offended him. In fact, God gave Job "twice as much as he had before." Thank God, there is healing and true prosperity in receiving and dispensing the forgiving grace of God.

The second illustration focuses on none other than the Lord Jesus Christ Himself. Being crucified for sinners, He looks out over the multitude and cries, "Father, forgive them; for they know not what they do." What a response from One who has suffered the wrath of wicked men.

He could have said, "I'll get you wicked devils, if it's the last thing I do." He could have sent all men to Hell and still been perfectly justified. But

He gave Himself to fully satisfy the sin-debt of sinners. Hallelujah, what a Saviour! The issue is this: If He could forgive wicked sinners like us, why won't we forgive other sinners too.

You can choose to be *bitter* or *better*. You can fret over your present circumstance and drive yourself right into despair, or you can face yourself in God's spiritual mirror (the Word of God) and deal squarely with your bitterness. If you do the latter, I guarantee you will be *better*. Don't wait, do it now.

"He that covereth his sins shall not prosper: but whoso confesseth and forsaketh them shall have mercy." (Prov. 28:13)

The story is told of a couple who got into a heated argument one evening. Their anger began to swell as they badgered each other with sharp and nasty words. In the midst of the fight, the wife left in a rage and got into the car. She decided to escape to the local store until things cooled off. Enroute, on a slick pavement, she lost control of the car and veered head-on into another vehicle and was instantly killed.

Think of it, she never returned home. The argument was never settled with her husband. Imagine the trauma he experienced as he stood next to her casket. He will take the pain of that experience to his grave.

Life is too short; let's deal with our pent up anger *now*. Tomorrow may be too late. Then, let's keep "short accounts" before God and others that we may learn to forgive. After all, we have been *forgiven*, so that now we can *forgive*.

END NOTES

* In Scripture texts with italicized words, the italics has been added by the publisher for emphasis.

1. Psa. 86:5
2. Col. 1:14
3. I John 1:9
4. Heb. 12:14-15
5. Psa. 66:18
6. Mark 11:25-26
7. Matt. 18:28. Repetition inferred from Greek text.
8. See Gen. 6:5; Jer. 17:9
9. Matt. 18:32-33
10. Note this term as it is later discussed and applied to the demonic depression suffered by unforgiving saints.
11. Dr. Redford Williams, "How to Defuse Your Anger." Article in *Bottom Line/Personal*, July 15, 1995, p. 11.
12. Idem
13. See also Prov. 14:30; 15:30; 16:24; and 17:22.
14. For a more detailed explanation of how mind affects the body, see chap. 7 of my book *Healing for the Mind*.
15. These terms are also discussed in *Healing for the Mind*.
16. Rev. 12:9-11 (Meditate on this passage.)
17. See this principle in the conversion of Zacchaeus (Luke 19:1-8).

Other Titles from Revival Literature

**Lordship Salvation:
Some Crucial Questions and Answers**
by Robert Lescelius

Marriage, Divorce, and Remarriage
by Theodore Epp

Religion, Our True Interest
by Thomas Watson

Your Personal Revival
by James A. Stewart

Heaven's Throne Gift
by James A. Stewart

The Spirit-Directed Life
by Robert Lescelius

Redeemed: Counsel for New Christians
by James A. Stewart

The Christian Life and How to Live It
by James A. Stewart

To order these and many other
helpful and encouraging books write to:

Revival Literature
P. O. Box 6068
Asheville, NC 28816